# Chili Recipes

## 25 Great Chili Recipes including vegetarian, Turkey, Seafood and Beef Recipes

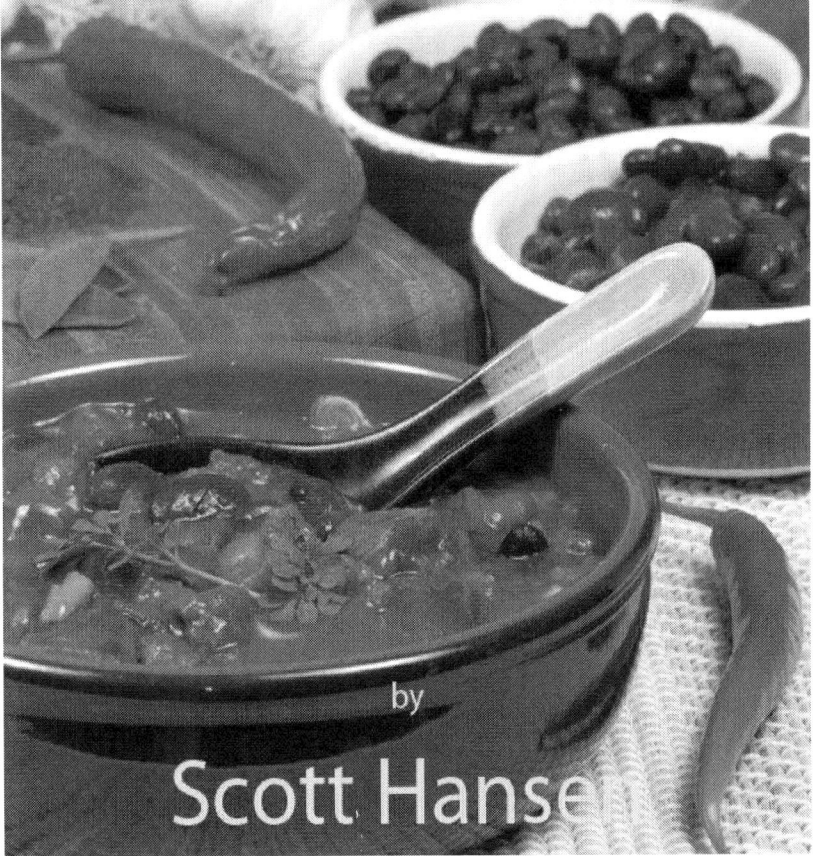

by

### Scott Hansen

Scott Hansen

scotthanse@gmail.com

# Contents

Introduction .................................................................7

1. Beef Chili..................................................................9

Beth's Pan Chili.............................................................9

Pan Chili Part II ...........................................................10

Wendy's-Style Chili ....................................................11

Chili with Peppers and Mushrooms.............................12

Slow Cooker Chili .......................................................13

Easy Pan Chili .............................................................14

Sahara Three Alarm Chili.............................................15

Best Chili Bar-None .....................................................16

Complex Beef Chili ......................................................18

Beef Chili Ambrosia.....................................................20

Beef Tip Chili ..............................................................22

Southern Chili Recipe...................................................24

Texas Champion Chili ..................................................26

Another Fine Chili ........................................................28

Yee-Haw Chili..............................................................30

2. Beef and Pork Chili .................................................33

Beef and Pork Chili ......................................................33

Italian Sausage and Beef Chili.....................................35

Great Chuck and Pork Chili..............................................37

Slow Cooker Pork Chili..................................................39

3. Seafood Chili ............................................................41

Seafood Chili ..............................................................41

4.  Turkey Chili............................................................43

Turkey Chili................................................................43

Turkey Chili Part II.......................................................45

Gobble-Gobble Chili ....................................................46

5. Vegetarian Chili........................................................49

Vegetarian Chili...........................................................49

6.  My Two Favorite Chilis .............................................50

President Reagan's Homemade Chili ala Scott .....................50

White Chicken Chili ......................................................52

# Introduction

I grew up in Minnesota, not a hotbed for great chili. When you think of Chili you think of Texas or any other Southwest state where cowboys ride horses and eat their dinners by a campfire. However, I grew up to like spicy food and food with flavor. While most of my family thinks ketchup is a spicy condiment, I travel down a different flavor path. When I went to Mexico the Mexican's I met were amazed at the amount of heat I liked to eat.

A great chili does not have to be spicy and burn the taste buds off of your tongue; rather it should be somewhat more complex and have deep and wonderful flavor profiles with it. I tend to cook my chili all day long to build up the flavors. But in today's world that is not always practical so I have included a chili recipe that takes about an hour to make.

Chili can be made many different ways and I have tried to include great recipes that will fulfill everyone's diet needs and tastes. I have included a vegetarian chili recipe, turkey chili recipes, beef recipes, and recipes that are made with other beef products. I know in Texas there is a strict NO BEANS rule for chili but I love beans so I have included recipes for those as well.

In my quest to find the perfect chili recipe I stumbled across a recipe that was loved by Ronald Reagan. I tweaked it a bit to suit my needs and I ended up making the best chili I have ever had in my life. It is not a hot chili at all; in fact it has an undercurrent of sweet in the flavor profile. It takes all day to make and it really tastes great if you make it the day before and refrigerate it overnight. The flavor the next day explodes in your mouth. I have included my favorite recipe in this collection.

I am not a professional cook, but I'm not bad. I have taken lessons from a friend who was schooled as a classically trained chef and her help made me a better cook myself. I love to experiment and change things up a bit, and I am not afraid to try things that are completely new and foreign to me. I cook for my family and friends and I learn more every day. If you follow my recipes and experiment a bit on your own, you too will be in the quest to find the perfect chili.

With that being said I have divided the book up into different sections based on what the main ingredients are in the chili. I put beef chili first because it is the most popular. I then created a section for chili made with poultry and I also have included one vegetarian chili recipe. My favorite chili, and Ronald Reagan's favorite chili is the last one I have listed.

Enjoy!

Scott Hansen

# 1. Beef Chili

## Beth's Pan Chili

This recipe was a chili that my mother-in-law made for her children when they were growing up. We in turn make it a lot for our kids, too. It is not a very spicy chili and it is you can make a pan in about an hour.

### Ingredients:
1 tbsp. vegetable oil
1 medium onion, chopped
1 lb. ground beef
1 (28 oz.) can stewed tomatoes
1 (28 oz.) can baked beans
1 (14 oz.) can of black beans
2 tbsp. chili powder
1 can of chopped green jalapeno chilies, or about three or four fresh ones

### Directions
1. Heat a large skillet with the vegetable oil. When the pan is heated add chopped onions. Sautee the onions in the large skillet for about four or five minutes. They should be translucent.
2. Add ground beef. Brown and break up into small pieces. Drain.
3. Add the rest of the ingredients and bring to a simmer. Do not drain the liquid from the canned goods. Taste. If you like it spicier add more chili powder.
4. Simmer for 20 minutes. Simmer longer if you want the flavors to get deeper.

# Pan Chili Part II

This recipe is also a pan chili but there is a big emphasis on beans. If you like beans then this recipe is for you. It is quick and easy to make and has a nice chili flavor. This recipe makes enough for two dinners for a family of four.

**Ingredients:**
1 tbsp. vegetable oil
1 medium onion, chopped
2 lbs. ground beef
3 cups tomato juice
1 (16 oz.) jar salsa
1 (16 oz.) can kidney beans, rinsed and drained
1 (15 oz.) can great northern beans, rinsed and drained
1 (15 oz.) can butter beans, rinsed and drained
1 (15 oz.) can black beans, rinsed and drained
1 (8 oz.) can tomato sauce
1 (6 oz.) can tomato paste
1 (4 oz.) can chopped green chilies
2 tbsp. chili powder

**Directions:**
1. In a large stock pot heat the vegetable oil.
2. Add chopped onions until translucent.
3. Add ground beef. Brown the ground beef and break up into small pieces. Drain.
4. Add rest of the ingredients.
5. Reduce heat and simmer uncovered for 15 minutes. Stir occasionally.

# Wendy's-Style Chili

This recipe is a close approximation of Wendy's Chili. If you like the chili at this fast-food restaurant then you will like this chili. This is a very easy recipe because there are two basic steps, browning the meat and adding the rest of the ingredients. This recipe takes longer to cook that the two recipes listed above but there is nothing better than the smell of cooking chili on a winter's day.

**Ingredients:**
2 lbs. ground beef
1 (29 oz.) can tomato sauce
1 (29 oz.) can kidney beans (with liquid)
1 (29 oz.) can pinto beans (with liquid)
1 medium onion, diced
2 jalapeno chilies, chopped
1 stalk celery, diced
3 medium tomatoes, chopped
3 tsps. cumin powder
3 tbsp. chili powder
2 tsp. black pepper
2 tsp. salt
2 cups water

**Directions:**
1. Brown ground beef in a skillet over medium heat. Break the ground beef into smaller pieces. Drain.
2. In a large stock pot, combine the beef plus all the remaining ingredients, and bring to a simmer over low heat.
3. Cook for 2 to 3 hours stirring every 15 minutes or so.
4. Serve.

# Chili with Peppers and Mushrooms

This recipe is fresh and tasty but it has mushrooms and peppers in it which some kids do not like.  It is a hearty beef chili that has more of a taco taste.  If you prefer, you can substitute chili powder for the taco seasoning to give this dish a more classic chili taste.  This chili is one of my favorites.

**Ingredients:**
1 lb. ground beef
1 small onion, chopped
1 cup chopped fresh mushrooms
1 small green pepper, chopped
1 small sweet red pepper, chopped
1 clove garlic, minced
2 cups water
1 (14.5 oz.) can diced tomatoes with green chilies, (not drained)
1 (1.25 oz.) package taco seasoning
1 (15 oz.) can great northern beans, rinsed and drained
1 (15 oz.) can black beans, rinsed and drained
1 (15 oz.) can pinto beans, rinsed and drained

**Directions:**
1.  In a large saucepan, cook beef and onion over medium heat until meat is no longer pink; drain.
2.  Add the mushrooms, peppers and garlic; cook and stir 3 minutes longer or until vegetables are almost tender.
3.  Add in the water, tomatoes and taco seasoning. Bring to boil.
4.  Reduce heat; simmer, uncovered, for 30 minutes.
5.  Add beans; simmer 30 minutes longer.

# Slow Cooker Chili

This recipe is designed to be made in a slow cooker. This means you get up in the morning, brown the meat and add the other ingredients and you let it cook for six hours. You can start this recipe, go to work and come home to hot chili.

**Ingredients:**
1 1/2 lbs. lean ground beef
2 (19 oz.) cans mixed beans, rinsed
2 cups salsa
1 (14 oz.) can no-salt-added tomato sauce
2 tbsp. chili powder
1 small onion, chopped
1 cup frozen corn, thawed, drained

**Directions:**
1. Brown meat; drain.
2. Put meat into slow cooker. Add the remaining ingredients; stir.
3. Cover with lid and cook on LOW 5 to 6 hours (or on HIGH 3 to 4 hours).
4. Stir before serving.

# Easy Pan Chili

This is another recipe that is easy to make and easy to serve and you use just one pan.  If you want a hotter chili use your favorite hot salsa.  The

**Ingredients:**
2 lbs. ground beef
1 small onion, chopped
1 tsp. ground black pepper
1/2 tsp. garlic salt
2 1/2 cups tomato sauce
1 (8 oz.) jar salsa
4 tbsp. chili powder
1 (15 oz.) can light red kidney beans
1 (15 oz.) can dark red kidney beans

**Directions:**
1. In a large saucepan over medium heat, combine the ground beef and the onion and sauté for 10 minutes, or until meat is browned and onion is tender. Break the meat up into small chunks.  Drain.
2. Add the rest of the ingredients.   Mix well.
3. Reduce heat to low and simmer for at least an hour, stirring occasionally.

# Sahara Three Alarm Chili

This chili packs a lot of punch and uses two kinds of chili powder plus chili grind ground beef, which is a bit coarser that normal ground beef.  If need be add extra water at the end to give the chili more of a liquid sauce.  This is a very flavorful and spicy chili, not meant for people who do not like the heat.

**Ingredients:**
1 tbsp. vegetable oil
1 small onion, chopped
2 lbs. course ground beef (chili grind)
1 (8 oz.) can tomato sauce
1 (14 oz.) can beef broth
2 tbsp. light chili powder
3 tbsp. dark chili powder
1 tbsp. garlic powder
½ tsp. salt
1 tbsp. ground cumin
1 tsp. cayenne pepper
½ tsp. black pepper
1 tsp. (or 1 cube) chicken stock granules
1 tsp. paprika
1 cup of water

**Directions:**
1. Add the oil, onion and beef to a large sauce pan.  Cook over medium heat until meat becomes a light brown.  Drain.
2. Add tomato sauce and beef broth.   Bring to a simmer and cook for 30 minutes.
3. Add light chili powder, dark chili powder, garlic powder, salt, ground cumin, cayenne pepper, black pepper, chicken granules, paprika, and water.  Stir ingredients.
4. Bring to a boil.  Reduce heat and simmer for 1 ½ to 2 hours, stirring occasionally.

# Best Chili Bar-None

This chili adds in a new ingredient to the beef, that is beef sirloin. This gives this chili a very meaty taste. Along with the beer and the other spices this chili is complex, and very tasty. I don't know if it is the best chili, I prefer Ronald Reagan's favorite chili at the end of this book, but it is absolutely near the top of the taste charts. It will take a little work to make this chili but when you do you will be rewarded.

**Ingredients:**
2 tsp. vegetable oil
2 medium onions, chopped
3 cloves garlic, minced
1 lb. lean ground beef
1 lb. beef sirloin, cubed
1 (14.5 oz.) can diced tomatoes
1 can of dark beer
2 (6 oz.) cans tomato paste
1 can beef broth
1/2 cup brown sugar
3 1/2 tbsp. chili sauce (in the ketchup aisle
1 tbsp. cumin
1 tbsp. cocoa
1 tsp. oregano
1 tsp. cayenne pepper
1 tsp. coriander
1 tsp. salt
4 (15 oz.) cans kidney beans
4 chili peppers, chopped

**Directions:**
1. Heat oil in large sauce pan.
2. Cook onions, garlic and meat until brown. Break up the ground beef into small pieces. Drain.
3. Add diced tomatoes, beer, tomato paste, and beef broth. Stir ingredients. Bring mixture up to a simmer.

4. Add brown sugar, chili sauce, cumin, cocoa, oregano, cayenne pepper, coriander, salt, 2 cans of kidney beans, and chili peppers. Mix well.
5. Reduce heat and simmer for 1 1/2 hours.
6. Add 2 remaining cans of kidney beans and simmer for another 30 minutes.

# Complex Beef Chili

This chili takes a bit more work but you get back what you put into it. You cannot simply add all the ingredients and let it go; it is more complex than that. You have to mix two separate bowls of spices that are added at different times. This chili is bursting with flavor. As with other more complex chili recipes, if you make it, refrigerate it, and reheat it the next day, the flavors really take hold. Take the extra time and make the extra effort and you will reap what you stew.

**Ingredients:**
2 lbs. chili grind beef chuck roast
1 tbsp. bacon grease
1 (14.5 oz.) can chicken broth
1 (14.5 oz.) can beef broth
1 (8 oz.) can tomato sauce
1 beef bouillon cube
1/2 tsp. light brown sugar

**Bowl 1**
3 tbsp. chili powder
1 tsp. garlic powder
2 tsp. onion powder
1/2 tsp. black pepper
1/2 tsp. salt
1/2 tsp. cayenne pepper

**Bowl 2**
3 tbsp. chili powder
1 tbsp. cumin
2 tsp. garlic powder
1/4 tsp. white pepper
1/2 tsp. oregano powder
½ tsp. basil

**Directions:**
1. Heat bacon grease in stock pot until very hot (smoking).

2. Add meat and brown.  Stir continuously so the beef does not burn.
3. Add chicken and beef broth and 1/2 of ingredients from bowl 1.
4. Cook covered at a medium boil for 45 minutes.  Uncover and stir every 10 minutes.
5. Add water as needed to maintain original liquid level in stock pot.
6. After 45 minutes, add the rest of ingredients from bowl 1, tomato sauce, and the ingredients from bowl 2, beef bouillon cube, and the light brown sugar.
7. Cook for 15 more minutes.
8. Ready to eat or refrigerate.  This tastes better the next day.

# Beef Chili Ambrosia

This chili is again a more complex chili that is full of different spices. This recipe will require about three hours of time to prepare and cook but the results are worth it. This chili has a complex footprint and the complexity makes this a fun dish to eat. As with most complex chili recipes, you can refrigerate the chili overnight and cook it the next day to bring even more flavor complexity to the table.

**Ingredients:**
**Step 1**
3 lbs. chili grind ground beef
1 (10.5 oz.) beef broth
1 (8 oz.) can tomato sauce
4 tbsp. onion flakes
2 tsp. beef base or instant beef bouillon
1 tsp. chicken base or instant chicken bouillon
1 tsp. garlic powder
2 tbsp. chili powder
2 tsp. Tabasco hot sauce

**Bowl 1**
1/2 tsp. black pepper
1/2 tsp. onion powder
1/2 tsp. garlic powder
1/2 tsp. white pepper
1 tbsp. ground cumin
1 tbsp. paprika
4 tbsp. chili powder
1/2 tsp. red pepper flakes

**Bowl 2**
3 tbsp. chili powder
1 tsp. ground cumin
1/2 tsp. red pepper flakes

**Directions:**

1. In a stock pot brown beef on medium heat.  Do not drain.
2. Add remaining ingredients from step one.
3. Bring to a boil; reduce heat, cover and simmer for 1 hour.  Stir every 15 minutes.
4. Add the spices from bowl 1.
5. Simmer for another hour.  Stir every 15 minutes.
6. Add the remaining spices from bowl 2.
7. Simmer 30 minutes.  Stir every 15 minutes.

# Beef Tip Chili

If you want to step up your main ingredients in chili from a ground beef or chuck, then this recipe is for you.  The main ingredient is beef tips, which are meaty and tender when cooked in this dish.   Besides being extremely flavorful this chili packs a punch.  Remember to wear gloves when cutting hot peppers and do not touch your eyes.

**Ingredients:**
2 lbs. beef tips
1 (18 oz.) bottle barbeque sauce
1 large onion, chopped
1 large green bell pepper, diced
2 tbsp. diced and seeded habanero pepper
2 pepperoncini, diced
1 tbsp. diced Serrano pepper
1 tbsp. diced fresh cayenne pepper
1 tbsp. diced pequin chili pepper
2 tbsp. diced jalapeno chili pepper
1 tsp. crushed red pepper flakes
1 tsp. ground cumin
1 tsp. paprika
1 tsp. dried oregano
3 tbsp. chili powder
2 lbs. ground beef
1 (14.5 oz.) can crushed tomatoes
1 (15 oz.) can pinto beans, drained

**Directions:**
1. Preheat an outdoor grill for high heat and lightly oil grate. Brush beef tips with barbeque sauce and grill 5 to 8 minutes on a side, or to desired doneness, brushing frequently with sauce. Set aside.
2. In a large stock pot over medium heat, cook onion, bell pepper, habanero pepper, pepperoncini, Serrano pepper, cayenne pepper, pequin pepper, and jalapeno peppers until onion is translucent.  About five minutes.

3. Stir in cumin, paprika, oregano and chili powder and cook until fragrant.
4. Add ground beef and cook until brown. Drain grease only.
5. Stir in tomatoes, any remaining barbeque sauce and beans.
6. Cut grilled tip steak into bite sized pieces and stir into chili as well.
7. Cook until thickened and flavors have blended and mixture is thoroughly heated; about 1 hour.
8. Thin with water if desired.

# Southern Chili Recipe

This recipe is complex and you can use either ground beef or you can use chuck tender cut into cubes. This is not an extremely hot chili but it does have a nice bite to it. Mexene Chili Powder is a brand that has been made in El Paso Texas for over 100 years and is a staple of Texas chili. You can order this online but if you do not want to do that you can also substitute your favorite chili powder. The brown sugar adds sweetness to a chili dish that has a hint of heat.

### Ingredients:
2-½ lbs. coarse ground beef or chuck tender cut into 3/8-inch cubes
1 tbsp. cooking oil
1 tsp. season salt
1 (8 oz.) can of tomato sauce
1 (14.5 oz.) can of beef broth

### Bowl 1
1 tbsp. Mexene Chili Powder
1-½ tbsp. onion granules
1 tbsp. paprika
2 tsp. garlic granules
½ tsp. salt
¼ tsp. black pepper
¼ tsp. cayenne
1 beef bouillon cube
1 chicken bouillon cube

### Bowl 2
5 tbsp. Mexene chili powder
3 tsp. cumin
1-½ tsp. garlic granules
¼ tsp. dark brown sugar
1 tsp. Tabasco sauce

### Directions:

1. Add the cooking oil, beef and salt to a stock pot and brown the meat.
2. Add tomato sauce and beef broth and bring to a boil.
3. Reduce heat and simmer for ½ hour.
4. Add the spices from bowl 1 into the stock pot.
5. Simmer for 1 hour.
6. Add water as needed to maintain liquid level.
7. Add bowl 2 spices to pot.
8. Simmer for ½ hour.
9. Add water as needed to maintain liquid level and consistency.

# Texas Champion Chili

Once again this is a complex recipe that will take several steps to complete if you want to do it right. Some of the ingredients are directly from Texas but should be available at a store near you. If not, we have included a substitute that will work for this recipe. If you choose the cubed beef chuck it may take a bit longer to cook in step three of the directions. Make sure the meat is tender.

**Ingredients:**
3 lbs. of cubed beef chuck tender (or chili grind)

**Bowl 1**
1 tbsp. vegetable oil
1 (8 oz.) can tomato sauce
½ (14.5 oz.) can chicken broth
1/2 tsp. cayenne pepper
2 tsp. chicken instant bouillon granules
1 tbsp. chili powder
2 Serrano peppers, chopped and seeded
1 (14.5 oz.) beef broth
1-1/2 tbsp. onion powder
2 tsp. beef instant bouillon
1 tsp. cumin

**Bowl 2**
3/4 tsp. white pepper
1 Packet Sazon Goya (Sazon Goya is a brand name Latino spice packet available at most stores; If you cannot find this look for a good taco seasoning mix)
1/4 tsp. salt
3 tbsp. chili powder
1 tsp. garlic powder
1 tbsp. cumin
2 tbsp. light chili powder

**Bowl 3**

1/4 tsp. brown sugar
1 tbsp. light chili powder
1 tsp. cumin

**Directions:**
1. Add oil to stock pot and heat.  Add beef and brown.  Drain.
2. Add bowl 1 to the stock pot and bring to a boil.
3. Reduce heat and simmer.  Cook for 1 hour.
4. Remove the peppers and add the ingredients from bowl 2.
5. Adjust liquid with remainder of chicken broth and water if needed. Cover and cook for 30 minutes.
6. Add the ingredients of bowl 3.
7. Simmer for 10 to 15 minutes.

# Another Fine Chili

This chili has Texas roots as well. These recipes has some kick to it and if it is not enough you can always add more heat with peppers. For a meatier chili, go with the cubed chuck. Cooking it in a hot pan will put a nice sear on the meat and when you cook it for an hour it will melt in your mouth.

**Ingredients:**
2-1/2 lbs. of chuck tender cubed or chili grind
1 tbsp. vegetable oil
½ tsp. salt
1 (14.5oz) can beef broth
1 (8 oz.) can tomato sauce

**Bowl 1**
1 tbsp. chili powder
1 tbsp. granulated onion
1 tsp. granulated garlic
1/2 tsp. cayenne pepper
1/4 tsp. ground jalapeno pepper
1 tsp. beef bouillon granules
1 tsp. chicken bouillon granules
1/2 tsp. salt

**Bowl 2**
4 tsp. cumin
1 tsp. granulated garlic
1/4 tsp. black pepper
1 package Sazon Goya (a Latino spice. If you do not have this in your local grocery store you can substitute a nice taco mix)
6 tbsp. chili powder
1/4 tsp. brown sugar

**Directions:**
1. Brown meat in vegetable oil and salt in a stock pot. Drain.
2. Add beef broth and tomato sauce.

3. Add water to cover meat plus an inch more. Add water as needed.
4. Bring to a boil then simmer for 30 minutes.
5. Add the contents of bowl 1.
6. Simmer for 1 hour. Make sure meat is tender. If needed cook longer.
7. Add ingredients from bowl 2.
8. Simmer for 1 hour.

# Yee-Haw Chili

This chili will explode in your mouth with tasty goodness. It will take about three hours to prepare and make the chili, and as always, if you refrigerate it overnight and serve it the next day, the flavors will become even more intense.

**Ingredients:**
2-1/2 lbs. beef chuck or round steak cut in 1/4" cubes
1 tbsp. vegetable oil
1 (8 oz.) can tomato sauce
1 (14.5 oz.) beef broth

**Bowl 1**
2 tbsp. Texas style chili powder
1 tbsp. onion powder
1/2 tsp. ground red pepper
2 tsp. beef base or instant bouillon granules
1 tsp. chicken base or instant bouillon granules
1/2 tsp. salt
1 tbsp. chili powder

**Bowl 2**
1 tbsp. ground cumin
2 tsp. garlic powder
3 tbsp. Texas style chili powder
1/4 tsp. ground black pepper

**Bowl 3**
1/2 tsp. salt
1/8 tsp. ground red pepper
1 tbsp. chili powder
1 tsp. ground cumin
1/2 tsp. onion powder

**Directions:**
1. In a stock pot heat oil and brown beef. Do not drain.

2. Add tomato sauce, beef broth and 2-1/4 cups water.
3. Add contents of bowl 1.
4. Bring to a boil; reduce heat and simmer 1-3/4 hours. You may need to add additional water if chili gets too thick.
5. Add contents of bowl 2.
6. Cover and simmer 30 minutes.
7. Add contents of bowl 3.
8. Cover and simmer for 15 minutes

# 2. Beef and Pork Chili

## Beef and Pork Chili

This chili mixes both ground beef and ground pork and it moves up on the complexity level in taste and ingredients. When you chop habanero or other hot peppers be sure to wear rubber gloves and do not touch your eyes. This chili is full of fresh ingredients that will really make the hot meter pop. The flavors are complex and get richer when you refrigerate this chili overnight. Your taste buds will thank you for the effort.

**Ingredients:**
1 lb. ground beef
1 lb. ground pork
2 tbsp. olive oil
1 medium onion, chopped
1 medium green bell pepper, chopped
1 habanero pepper, seeded and minced
2 jalapeno peppers, seeded and minced
3 cloves of garlic, minced
3 chopped green scallions
3 (15 oz.) cans chili beans
1 (14.5 oz.) can diced tomatoes
1 (6 oz.) can tomato paste
1 (8 oz.) can tomato sauce
1 (12 oz.) bottle lager-style beer
1 cup water
2 tbsp. cornmeal
1/4 cup chili powder
1 tbsp. ground cumin
1 tsp. garlic powder
1/2 tsp. cayenne pepper
1 tbsp. salt
1 1/2 tsp. ground black pepper

**Directions:**

1. Cook ground beef and pork in a large skillet over medium-high heat until the meat is crumbly, evenly browned, and no longer pink. Drain.
2. While the meat is browning, heat the olive oil in a large pot over medium heat. Stir in the onion, green pepper, habanero pepper, jalapeno peppers, and garlic.
3. Cook and stir until the onion has softened and turned translucent, about 5 minutes.
4. Add the drained meat into the onion and peppers mixture along with the green scallions, chili beans, diced tomatoes, tomato paste, tomato sauce, beer, and water. Stir together until well-mixed.
5. Add the cornmeal, chili powder, cumin, garlic powder, cayenne pepper, salt, and black pepper. Stir ingredients.
6. Bring to a simmer over medium heat. Once the mixture starts to boil reduce heat to medium-low. Simmer at least 2 hours, stirring occasionally.
7. Refrigerate overnight.
8. Reheat the chili the next day and let it simmer for about 30 minutes.

# Italian Sausage and Beef Chili

This chili is the uses ground chuck, although ground beef can be substituted, along with Italian sausage which can be purchased in the same form as ground beef. For extra kick get the hot Italian sausage. This chili had a lot of beans in it as well and delivers a complex taste. It should cook for at least two hours and it is even better if you refrigerate it and serve it the next day.

**Ingredients:**
2 lbs. ground beef chuck
1 lb. bulk Italian sausage
3 (15 oz.) cans of chili beans, drained
1 (15 oz.) can chili beans in spicy sauce
2 (28 oz.) cans diced tomatoes with juice
1 (6 oz.) can tomato paste
1 large onion, chopped
3 stalks celery, chopped
1 green bell pepper, seeded and chopped
1 red bell pepper, seeded and chopped
2 green chili peppers, seeded and chopped
1 tbsp. bacon bits
4 cubes beef bouillon
1/2 cup beer
1/4 cup chili powder
1 tbsp. Worcestershire sauce
1 tbsp. minced garlic
1 tbsp. dried oregano
2 tsp. ground cumin
2 tsp. Tabasco sauce
1 tsp. dried basil
1 tsp. salt
1 tsp. ground black pepper
1 tsp. cayenne pepper
1 tsp. paprika
1 tsp. sugar

**Directions:**

1. Add ground chuck and Italian sausage to a large stock pot over medium-high heat. Crumble the ground chuck and sausage, and cook until evenly browned. Drain.
2. Pour in the chili beans, spicy chili beans, diced tomatoes and tomato paste and stir.
3. Add the onion, celery, green and red bell peppers, chili peppers, bacon bits, bouillon, and beer.  Stir and bring to a simmer.
4. Season with chili powder, Worcestershire sauce, minced garlic, oregano, cumin, Tabasco sauce, basil, salt, pepper, cayenne pepper, paprika, and sugar. Stir to blend, then cover and simmer over low heat for at least 2 hours, stirring occasionally.
5. After 2 hours, taste, and adjust salt, pepper, and chili powder if necessary. The longer the chili simmers, the better it will taste. Remove from heat and serve, or refrigerate, and serve the next day.   For a deeper and richer flavor refrigerate and serve the next day.

# Great Chuck and Pork Chili

This chili also combines ground chuck and ground pork and if you want you can substitute ground beef for ground chuck.  With the cornmeal and flower added at the end it help firm up the chili and gives it a stew-like consistency.  The flavors are bold and fresh and this recipe can be made in about three hours.

**Ingredients:**
2 1/2 lbs. ground chuck
1 lb. lean ground pork
1 tbsp. vegetable oil
4 garlic cloves, chopped
1 medium onion, chopped
1 (8 oz.) can tomato sauce
1 cup water
1 (12 oz.) can beer
3 tbsp. chili powder
2 tbsp. (or 6 cubes) instant beef bouillon
2 tbsp. ground cumin
2 tsp. paprika
2 tsp. ground oregano
2 tsp. sugar
1/2 tsp. coriander, ground
1 tsp. unsweetened cocoa
1/2 tsp. hot sauce
1 tsp. cornmeal
1 tsp. flour
1 tsp. warm water

**Directions:**
1. In a large saucepan brown the ground chuck and pork over medium heat until brown.  Drain.
2. Remove cooked meat and set aside.
3 Add the vegetable oil, garlic and onion.  Cook and stir until translucent and tender, about 5 minutes.

4. Add meat, tomato sauce, water, beer, chili powder, bouillon, cumin, paprika, ground oregano, sugar, coriander, cocoa, and hot sauce. Mix well.

5. Bring to a boil then reduce heat and simmer, covered, for 2 hours.

6. In a small bowl stir together the cornmeal, flour, and warm water. Mix well.

7. Stir mixture into chili and cook, covered, for an additional 20 minutes.

# Slow Cooker Pork Chili

This recipe is for a slow cooker and is the only recipe in this book to use pork exclusively. The directions are in two parts. First, you will need to roast your vegetables and chilies. Roasting will bring out the intensity of the flavors before you add it to the crock pot. The second part of the directions involve cooking the pork in a frying pan and then transferring it to a slow cooker. This is an all-day cooking chili. I have not personally tried this specific recipe because I am not a fan of pork. I have been told it is delicious.

**Ingredients Part 1:**
4 fresh tomatillos - husked, peeled, and halved
3 Anaheim chili peppers - seeded and halved
3 jalapeno peppers - seeded and halved lengthwise
1 medium onion, halved
1 green bell pepper, seeded and halved lengthwise
1 tbsp. olive oil, or as needed
salt to taste

**Directions Part 1:**
1. Preheat oven to 425 degrees.
2. Arrange the halved tomatillos, Anaheim chili, jalapenos, onion, and green bell pepper on a baking sheet. Drizzle the vegetables with 1 tbsp. of olive oil.
3. Roast the vegetables until they begin to show brown spots, about 30 minutes. Allow to cool, and then chop vegetables into bite-size pieces.

**Ingredients Part 2:**
1 tbsp. olive oil
1 1/2 cups pork shoulder, cut into 1-inch chunks
½ tsp. salt
1 tsp. ground black pepper
2 tomatoes, chopped
4 cloves garlic, chopped
1 beef bouillon cube

1/2 (12 oz.) can or bottle, lager-style beer
2 tbsp. chopped fresh oregano
1 tbsp. chopped fresh parsley
1 tbsp. ground cumin
1 tsp. chili powder
4 oz. cream cheese at room temperature

**Directions Part 2:**
1. Heat olive oil in a large skillet over high heat.
2. Pan-fry the pork until browned, sprinkling the meat with salt and black pepper as it cooks.  About 12 minutes.
3. Transfer the pork cubes to a slow cooker, and stir in the roasted vegetables.
4. Mix in the tomatoes, garlic, beef bouillon cube, beer, oregano, parsley, cumin, and chili powder. Set the cooker on Low, cover, and cook until the pork is very tender, about 4 to 6 hours.
5. About 1/2 hour before serving, place the cream cheese into a bowl, and stir in about 1 tbsp. of the chili liquid until thoroughly combined. Continue stirring in chili broth, a tbsp. at a time, until the cream cheese is almost a liquid. Stir the cream cheese mixture back into the chili.

# 3. Seafood Chili

## Seafood Chili

Seafood and chili are not synonymous. In fact I bet you would be hard pressed to find this on any menu in any restaurant in America. Most people either like chili and meat or seafood but they do not want to mix the two. This recipe cuts out the meat entirely and adds seafood. This is probably the most labor intense chili recipe in the book. You must refrigerate the chili overnight and you must take your time and add the seafood as indicated. You do not want overcooked seafood. If you follow the directions you will get a seafood version of chili. Enjoy!

### Ingredients:
4 tbsp. olive oil
2 small onions, chopped
2 leeks, white part only, chopped
10 garlic cloves, minced
5 tsp. dried oregano
1 (35 oz.) can Italian plum tomatoes, not drained
1 (16 oz.) can clam juice
2 cups dry red wine
1/2 cup chili powder
5 tsp. toasted cumin seed
1 tbsp. salt
1 tsp. cayenne pepper
2 medium red bell peppers, chopped
12 Littleneck clams
12 mussels, scrubbed and debearded
1 1/2 lb. grouper cut into 1 inch pieces
12 large shrimp, peeled and deveined
3/4 lb. Bay scallops
Fresh cilantro for serving

### Directions:
1. Heat oil in heavy saucepan over low heat.

2. Add onions and leeks. Cover and cook until tender, usually about 15 minutes.
3. Add garlic and oregano, and cook another 10 minutes.
4. Add tomatoes, breaking up large pieces with a spatula. Stir in the clam juice, wine, chili powder, cumin, salt and cayenne pepper. Slowly bring to a boil. Reduce heat and simmer, partially covered for 1 hour.
5. Add bell peppers and simmer for 20 minutes.
6. Refrigerate overnight.
7. Bring sauce to a boil. Reduce heat to a brisk simmer.
8. Add clams and mussels. Cover and cook until shellfish open, approximately 5 to 10 minutes.
9. Discard any shellfish that do not open.
10. Gently stir in grouper and shrimp. Cover and simmer for 2 minutes.
11. Add scallops. Cover and simmer until fish is just opaque, about 3 minutes.
12. Top with cilantro and serve.

# 4.  Turkey Chili

## Turkey Chili

This recipe uses turkey instead of beef, if you want to make a chili that is a little healthier for you.  It has a nice robust taste highlighted by the sautéed vegetables you add at the end.   This recipe can be made in about an hour for a quick and delicious meal.

**Ingredients:**
3 tbsp. vegetable oil, divided
1 1/2 lbs. ground turkey
1 (1 oz.) package taco seasoning mix
1 tsp. ground coriander
1 tsp. dried oregano
1 tsp. chili pepper flakes
2 tbsp. tomato paste
1 (14.5 oz.) can beef broth
1 (7 oz.) can salsa
1 (14.5 oz.) can crushed tomatoes, or coarsely chopped tomatoes packed in puree
1 (7 oz.) can chopped green chili peppers
1 medium onion, finely chopped
1 green bell pepper, diced
3 medium zucchini, halved lengthwise and sliced

**Directions:**
1.   Heat 1 tbsp. of oil in a large stock pot over medium-high heat.
2.   Crumble turkey into the pot, stirring with a wooden spoon to break apart as much as possible.
3.   Season with taco seasoning mix, coriander, oregano, chili flakes, and tomato paste, and mix until meat is evenly coated with seasonings.
4.   Continue cooking, reducing heat if necessary, until turkey is well browned.

5. Pour in beef broth, and simmer to reduce liquid slightly, about 5 minutes.
6. Add salsa, tomatoes, and green chilies, and continue cooking at a simmer for 10 minutes. Adjust the thickness at any time you feel necessary by adding water.
7. While chili is still cooking, heat one tbsp. of oil in a large skillet over medium-high heat. Cook onion and green bell pepper, stirring occasionally for 5 minutes, or until onion is translucent and bell pepper is lightly browned. Add onion and bell pepper to the chili, and continue cooking at a very low simmer.
8. In the same skillet, heat the remaining tbsp. of oil over medium-high heat. Add the zucchini, and cook stirring occasionally, for 5 minutes, or until lightly browned.
9. Add the zucchini to the chili, reduce heat, and continue cooking 15 minutes more. Adjust the consistency with water as needed.

# Turkey Chili Part II

This recipe for turkey chili has fewer vegetables than the first recipe. It is a recipe that is easy to make and with prep work can be completed in about an hour and a half. If you desire use low-fat sour cream or low-fat yogurt to top it off to help give it that authentic taste.

## Ingredients:
2 cups dry lentils
2 (32 oz.) cans of vegetable broth
2 tbsp. extra-virgin olive oil
4 cloves garlic, minced
1 large onion, chopped
2 stalks celery, chopped
1 lb. turkey sausage
2 tomatoes, peeled, seeded, and chopped
1 tsp. ground turmeric
1 tsp. ground cumin
1/2 tsp. dried thyme leaves
1 pinch crushed red pepper flakes
sea salt to taste

## Directions:
1. Bring lentils and vegetable broth to a boil in a large stock pot over high heat. Reduce heat to medium, and simmer for 10 minutes.
2. Meanwhile, heat the olive oil in a large skillet over medium-high heat. Stir in the garlic, onion, celery, and sausage; cook and stir until the sausage is crumbly and no longer pink, about 10 minutes.
3. Stir in tomatoes, turmeric, cumin, thyme, and red pepper flakes; cook 5 minutes more.
4. Stir the sausage mixture into the simmering lentils. Continue simmering until the lentils are tender, 20 to 30 minutes.
5. Season to taste with salt.

# Gobble-Gobble Chili

This turkey recipe is more complex than the first two recipes. This is closer to real, down-home chili except there is no beef in it. The peppers you cut will be hot so wear gloves and do not rub your eyes. The recipe has a lot of ingredients but when cooked together they marry well and you end up with a chili that has a wonderful and complex taste profile.

**Ingredients:**
2 tbsp. olive oil
1 medium onion, chopped
5 cloves garlic, minced
2 small green bell peppers, seeded and chopped
1 habanero pepper, seeded and chopped
2 lbs. lean ground turkey
2 tbsp. chili powder
2 tsp. red pepper flakes
1 tbsp. paprika
1 tbsp. ground cumin
2 tsp. dried oregano
1 tsp. ground black pepper
1 (1 oz.) envelope instant hot chocolate mix
2 tsp. seasoned salt
1 tbsp. Worcestershire sauce
1 tsp. liquid smoke flavoring
2 (14.5 oz.) cans diced tomatoes with green chili peppers, drained
1 (8 oz.) can tomato sauce
1 (15 oz.) can kidney beans, drained
1 (12 oz.) bottle or can of beer
1/2 cup canned whole kernel corn
1 tbsp. hot pepper sauce

**Directions:**
1. Heat the olive oil in a large saucepan over medium heat.
2. Add the onion, garlic, green peppers and habanero peppers; cook and stir until the onion is transparent, about five minutes.

3. Push these to one side of the pot, and crumble in the ground turkey. Cover, and cook for about 10 minutes, stirring occasionally, until the meat is no longer pink. Make sure nothing burns.
4. Season with chili powder, red pepper flakes, paprika, cumin, oregano, pepper, hot cocoa mix and seasoned salt.
5. Stir in Worcestershire sauce, liquid smoke, diced tomatoes with green chilies, tomato sauce and kidney beans.
6. Add the beer. Partially cover the pan, and simmer over medium heat for about 50 minutes, stirring occasionally.
7. Mix in the corn and hot pepper sauce, and simmer for about 10 more minutes.

# 5. Vegetarian Chili

## Vegetarian Chili

This vegetarian chili is more like a vegetable soup with chili flavors. The beans give the dish some protein and weight. When you add the ingredients together you get a healthy and tasty dish that the whole family will enjoy.

**Ingredients:**
3 Tbsp. olive oil
1 1/2 cups chopped onion
8 large garlic cloves, chopped
2 (19 oz.) cans red kidney beans
2 (19 oz.) cans dark red kidney beans
1 envelope taco seasoning or 1/4 cup taco seasoning
1 tsp. dried basil
1/2 tsp. dried oregano
1/2 tsp. dried thyme
1 (15oz.) can tomato sauce
3 cups vegetable broth
1 (6 oz.) can tomato paste

**Directions:**
1. Heat oil in heavy saucepan over medium-high heat.
2. Add onions and garlic. Sauté about 5 minutes or until onions are translucent.
3. Add beans, taco seasoning, basil, oregano, and thyme. Stir 2 minutes.
4. Mix in tomato sauce, chicken broth and tomato paste.
5. Simmer until thickened to desired consistency, stirring occasionally to prevent sticking, about one-and-a-half-hours.
6. Refrigerate until cold then reheat over low when ready to serve.

# 6. My Two Favorite Chilis

## President Reagan's Homemade Chili ala Scott

I was taught this recipe at a cooking demonstration and I modified it a bit to my liking. I have entered this chili in a couple of local office contests and both times everyone thought it was the best chili. The chili has deep, rich and complex flavors. There is a mixture of both sweet and hot. The orange zest adds a little citrus flavor. The beef bones really help add to the beef flavor and complexity. I promise when you make this chili it will be your favorite and it will be worth it.

**Ingredients:**
2 lbs. ground beef
½ cup bacon drippings (or cook 1 lb. bacon and use the grease from this)
1 Package of beef bones (sliced like dog treats) from the butcher
2 small onions, chopped
4 garlic cloves, chopped
1 red pepper, chopped
1 yellow pepper chopped
2 tbsp. of chili powder
1 tbsp. of Anso chili powder
2 cups red wine
1 tbsp. of salt
1 tbsp. beef base
2 (14 oz.) cans of chopped tomatoes
1 tbsp. sugar
2 tbsp. of brown sugar
1 (14.5 oz.) can northern beans
1 (14.5 oz.) can black beans
1 orange for orange zest

**Directions:**
1. Preheat oven to 425.
2. Brown the beef and set aside.

3. If cooking bacon to get the bacon grease, spread the bacon out into two cake pans and cook bacon until it is done how you like it. Turn over midway. For crisp bacon this will take about 20 minutes total. Set bacon aside but use the bacon grease for the next step.
4. Turn oven to broil and when the broiler is heated put in beef bones on a cookie sheet for 3 minutes each side.
5. Using a stock pot melt bacon drippings (or use fresh bacon grease). When hot, add onions and sweat the onions over low heat (until onions are translucent), about 5 minutes.
6. Add both garlic cloves and both peppers. Cook for a couple of minutes over low heat to soften the peppers a bit and build the flavor.
7. Add beef bones and add ground beef in sauté mixture. Stir.
8. Add chili powders and stir until mixture is well mixed.
9. Add red wine, salt, beef base, tomatoes and sugars (make sure to really break up and stir in brown sugar).
10. Zest the orange and add the zest from 1 orange to the mixture.
11. Simmer covered for 20 minutes stirring often.
12. Open northern beans and black beans and drain and rinse.
13. Add beans to chili mixture after cooking above for 20 minutes.
14. Simmer chili for an hour, stirring gently from time to time.
15. Take out beef bones. Test for flavor.
16. To enhance the flavors of the chili let it cool and refrigerate overnight. Reheat the next day.

# White Chicken Chili

This is my wife's favorite chili and our friends love it too. It is very unlike the rest of the chili in this book because it is white, it is made of chicken, and because my wife is from Wisconsin it has a lot of cheese in it. It is like a thick and hearty soup in many ways.

## Ingredients
2 tbsp. olive oil
6 cloves of garlic
2 small onions, chopped
3 tbsp. flour
4 cups of cooked chicken diced or shredded (2.5 to 3 lbs. of chicken breast works well)
1 cup dry white wine
4 cups of chicken broth
1 tsp. powdered ginger
3 tsp. cumin
2 bay leaves (optional)
4 (14.5 oz. cans) Great Northern beans, undrained
2 (4 oz. cans) diced green chilies
1 (4 oz. can) diced jalapenos
2 (8 oz. blocks or packages) Monterey Jack cheese, grated
2 (8 oz. blocks or packages) pepper jack cheese, grated
Salt, pepper and oregano to taste

## Directions
1. Put olive oil in large stock pot over medium heat until hot
2. Add garlic and onions and cook until translucent, about five minutes
3. Add flour to mixture to thicken
4. Add all the remaining ingredients except for the cheese
5. Simmer for three hours on low heat
6. Add cheese and continue to simmer on low. Do not put heat on too high because it will burn the cheese

7. Ready to serve when the cheese completely melts, about ½ hour

Please visit our fan page at:

http://www.facebook.com/pages/Chili-Recipes/202293256527245

25534823R00031

Printed in Great Britain
by Amazon